INTERESTING WAYS TO TEACH

253 Ideas

For Your Teaching

Withdrawn

T016055

Accession Number....27,642....©

Class Number......374 · 13..........

253 Ideas
for your teaching

Graham Gibbs
Professor and Head,
Oxford Centre for Staff Development,
Oxford Brookes University

Trevor Habeshaw
Educational Consultant,
TES Associates, Bristol
and
University of Exeter

LIBRARY
BISHOP BURTON COLLEGE
BEVERLEY HU17 8QG

First published in 1988 by
Technical and Educational Services Ltd.,
37 Ravenswood Road
Bristol BS6 6BW
UK

Second Edition   1990
Third Edition   1992
Third Edition   1995

© 1988, 1990, 1995 Graham Gibbs & Trevor Habeshaw

ISBN 0 947885 38 2

Printed in Great Britain by
The Cromwell Press, Broughton Gifford
Wiltshire, U.K.   .

Distributed by
Plymbridge Distribution Ltd, Estover Road, Plymouth PL6 7PZ
telephone (01752) 695745   fax (01752) 695699

Contents

Books from Technical & Educational Services

The 53 series
53 Interesting things to do in your lectures
53 Interesting things to do in your seminars and tutorials
53 Interesting ways to assess your students
53 Interesting ways of helping your students to study
53 Interesting communication exercises for science students
53 Interesting ways to appraise your teaching
53 Interesting ways to promote equal opportunities in education
53 Interesting ways to teach mathematics
53 Interesting ways to write open learning materials
53 Interesting activities for open learning courses
53 Problems with large classes: *Making the best of a bad job*
53 Questions and answers about modules and semesters

Interesting ways to teach
Preparing to teach: *An introduction to effective teaching in higher education*
253 Ideas for your teaching
Interesting ways to teach: *12 Do-it-yourself staff development exercises*
Creating a teaching profile

Other titles
Getting the most from your data: *Practical ideas on how to analyse qualitative data*
Writing study guides
Improving the quality of student learning
HMA Stationery Ltd. *(an open & flexible learning study pack)*

Preface

This book was originally written to support special weeks devoted to teaching innovations at Oxford, Bristol and North London Polytechnics in 1988. It is based on a booklet produced to support similar "Non-Traditional Teaching" weeks at Oxford and Bristol Polytechnics in 1987. It has proved a quick and effective way of giving teachers ideas for enlivening their teaching and their students' learning.

Many of the ideas here are drawn from other books in the *Interesting Ways To Teach* series published by TES Ltd. The contents of these books are listed in the relevant sections so that you can find fuller descriptions of the rationale and methodology of ideas which interest you.

These 253 ideas are offered to help you to generate your own ideas for innovations in your teaching. Some have been well tried and tested – you may have tried them yourself. Others are untried and may seem new, or even plain odd. Some involve substantial preparation and some risk. Others can be tried on the spur of the moment with safety and without much effort. We hope that amongst such a large collection you will find something which attracts you and which seems feasible.

Those who have helped in the generation of ideas in this book include John Cowan, Director of the Open University in Scotland; David Jaques, Head of the Educational Methods Unit, Oxford Brookes University; and Di Steeds, Subeditor of the European Journal of Biochemistry. Their help and creativity is gratefully acknowledged.

1   Lectures

1 Overview

Condense the whole course/module/year into one lecture to give as broad an overview as possible as a way of helping students to integrate their knowledge. Tape record the lecture and use extracts as "triggers" in tutorials or other lectures.

2 Audiotape

Tape record your lecture and put the tape in the library for students to listen to at their leisure: for revision purposes, for next year, for students on other courses, for when you drop the lecture from the course.

3 Team teaching

Lecture with a colleague: not just 30 minutes each, but taking several turns each, preferably responding to and moving on from each other. Students appreciate disagreements and different perspectives, so you don't have to plan for perfect co-ordination. Combine classes from two courses/modules to avoid extra work.

4 Problems

Approach every piece of subject matter as a problem to be solved. Invite students to solve or understand the problem and then suggest your solutions and those of others.

5 Video

Lecture to a video camera. Don't bother with fancy techniques, graphics, etc., because that can make it time consuming. Prepare handouts where students need to see diagrams or other visual detail. In class, show the video and stop and start the tape at the request of the students, who ask for time to take notes, ask questions, discuss points etc as they wish. It is easier to stop a video than a lecturer!

6   Student teachers

Teams of three students prepare and deliver the lecture you would have given. Give them help in the form of your old notes, your OHP transparencies and slides etc.   Have a "dress rehearsal" to check they can cope OK.   During their presentation either stay away or keep a low profile or you may put the students off.

7   Role play lectures

Take the role of a prominent theorist, historical figure, character in literature, person in a case study, etc., and talk from their perspective.   A more powerful impact can be achieved by team teaching with lecturers taking on different roles of people who have been in conflict in their views (but who were not alive at the same time or who never met).

8   Memory

Students take no notes at all, but listen carefully instead. When technical details are important, require no note taking for 10 minute sections, each followed by time to take notes from memory. Improves student attention, speeds your lecturing (compared with dictation!), improves students' memory of the lecture.

9   Listening

Students shut their eyes and just listen for 10 minute periods. This leads to either greater reflectiveness or sleep, depending on your talent!

10   Lecture swop

Swop your lecture with that of a colleague in a different subject area and both of you then lecture on an unfamiliar topic. This can lead to useful simplification and avoid overwhelming detail. It can be most helpful to students when you share your problems coping with an unfamiliar topic, e.g. *"I have found this difficult to grasp and explain. What I think it means is . . . but the problem I have with it is . . . "* It can be very useful to students to see how experienced learners tackle new topics.

11   Orientation

Use music, slides, posters or a video to create an atmosphere appropriate for the lecture or to portray without words what the lecture will be about at the start. Give students time to reflect back over the course so far and leave their previous class behind in their minds before you start.

12   Student notes

Look at students' notes after your lecture to identify which bits they got and which bits they didn't. Ask a couple of students to use carbon paper so that you can take a copy. Spend 5 minutes on the omissions and errors at the start of the next lecture. Alternatively, have a break after 25 minutes and look at their notes. Clear up what look like problems before you proceed with the lecture.

13   Uncompleted handouts

Use handouts with gaps in them for students to write in during the lecture: labels of diagrams and axes of graphs, formulae, open ended sections etc. Give students time to fill in these sections from your talk or overhead projector transparencies. This keeps students active and allows them to personalise their handouts whilst making less demand on them than having to write their own notes without the help of handouts.

14   OHP

Try using the overhead projector in new ways. Have transparencies redone smartly by your audio visual service. Use overlays and masks to reveal information in a controlled and focused way. Produce enlarged photocopies of recent press articles/ photos/diagrams on to transparencies. Produce handouts which are the same as your complex transparencies or which leave bits of them out (as in 13 above). Use two OHPs side by side: one for displaying the structure of the lecture and where you have got to, and the other for the details.

15   Objectives

Try stating at the start: "At the end of this lecture you will be able to . . .". Only allow yourself verbs which operationalise cognitive activities: ie. to describe, to prove, to solve, to recommend, are OK, but to understand, to grasp, are not OK because they cannot be tested.

16   Finish with a test

Check what students have learned by giving a short test at the end to be 'marked' by the students themselves or their neighbours. Link to objectives (15 above). Warning that a test will be given will improve attention, even if the test doesn't count for anything.

17   Advance organiser

Use an example, an illustration, a summary, a diagram, a map, chart or other graphic representation of the subject at the start to give students a framework into which they can organise subsequent content.

18   Last week, next week

Start by reviewing what was covered last time: not just the topic, but a two minute summary. Display a summary OHP while students are settling down. Finish by outlining what will come next: again not too briefly. You can use an advance organiser for this (see **17** above). Display an OHP which summarises the content of your next lecture as they pack up.

19 Mini-lectures

Never lecture for more than 15 minutes at a time. Remember that students' attention drops to a dismal low after about 20 minutes. Use the rest of the time for tasks: problems, note taking in silence, reading, discussion in pairs, or for knocking off for a coffee.

20 Breaks

Give frequent brief breaks: 30 seconds silence to catch up with notes, one minute to stand up and stretch your legs, two minutes to confer with neighbours and so on. The longer you have lectures without a break, the longer the break needs to be: one minute after 10, two after 20, ten after 60.

21 Buzz groups

After 15 minutes set students a problem or discussion question to tackle in pairs. Expecting one or two pairs to report what they have concluded makes sure they take the task seriously. 3 minutes of lively buzz sets students up to be able to listen to more lecturing as well as giving them an opportunity to apply what you have already covered.

22 Pyramid

Before working in pairs (see **21**, Buzz Groups), students should work alone for a minute or so. After working in pairs they draw conclusions in fours. You then pool conclusions from the fours on an OHP for all to see what the other groups have been up to. In this way it is possible to handle large group discussions even in a large lecture theatre. Can even be done with 1200 students, taking the group size up to 8 before the plenary stage.

23 Quiet time

Allow periods of up to 5 minutes for quiet reflection: to develop notes, prepare questions, review earlier sections of the course. The only rule is that no-one speaks for any reason whatsoever.

24 The three most important things . . .

5 minutes from the end, ask students to write down the three most important things from the lecture: either from memory or allowing them to look through their notes. Write down your own three on a transparency, then project it for all to see. See how many got all three, two, one or none. Good to get feedback, but also to give students feedback: it helps them to see what you are really on about and improves their notes next time.

25 "Are there any questions?"

None of us has much success with this question. By the time students have formulated a question, you have moved on, or they are hesitant to display their ignorance. Give them a minute on their own to write down the question(s) that they would really like an answer to. Then ask them to address this question to their neighbours to try and sort out amongst themselves. Then field the outstanding questions which have not been satisfactorily dealt with. By this time they will have well formulated questions which they know are not trivial or easy and they usually call them out without hesitation.

26 Where is the music in forensic chemistry?

Well, where is it? Give a lecture on what it is which intrigues and inspires you in your life as a scholar.

27 Themes

The whole course adopts a theme for the week and slants every lecture towards that theme in some way. General themes could be: racism, sexism, inequality, alternative technology, information technology, careers.

28   Ban

Ban all use of blackboards: no chalk and talk. Try something else for a change.

29   Flipchart

Try using flipchart paper instead of a chalkboard or OHP and display each completed sheet on the wall so that all your writing is visible at once.

30   Head of department

Introduce your students to your Head by inviting her (or him) to give a lecture or chair a seminar on your course. Encourage your Head to teach and meet as many students as possible during the week. Do the same with your Deans and Directorate or Vice Chancellor.

31   Clothes

Wear something different and behave differently as a result. Cut across the conventions which normally operate in your lectures. If you normally wear tweeds and speak from a lectern, come in jeans and sit on the corner of the front bench. If you normally dress sloppily and slouch around chatting, come in a suit and give a snappy lecture with smart overhead transparencies and typed handouts. Shock the students.

LIBRARY
BISHOP BURTON COLLEGE
BEVERLEY HU17 8QG

A wider range of more detailed descriptions of interesting ways to teach in lectures can be found in *53 Interesting things to do in your lectures*, the contents of which are listed below.

STRUCTURING THE PROCESS

1 Briefing
2 Flagging
3 Ground rules
4 Students' questions
5 Orientation

IMPROVING STUDENTS' NOTES

6 Swop
7 Memory
8 Tape recording
9 "Now write this down"
10 Filing
11 Review
12 Looking at students' notes

USING HANDOUTS

13 Theme summary
14 Diagrams
15 Problems
16 Questions
17 Uncompleted handouts
18 Article
19 Reading guide

STRUCTURING AND SUMMARISING CONTENT

20 Structuring
21 Objectives
22 Advance organiser
23 Displaying the structure
24 Progressive structuring
25 Repetition
26 Simultaneous messages
27 "The three most important things . . ."

LINKING LECTURES

HOLDING ATTENTION

ACTIVE LEARNING DURING LECTURES

CHECKING ON LEARNING

Information on how to order *53 Interesting things to do in your lectures* can be found at the end of the book.

2   Seminars

1 Leave the room

After setting the seminar up and briefing your students, simply leave the room. Either promise to come back at a particular time – perhaps after 35 minutes – or stay in your nearby office until they come and request that you return. It could be a long wait! Students usually enjoy the opportunity of uninterrupted discussion which is invariably more lively and involves more of the students than when you are present. Use the last two minutes of the seminar to discuss their experience and ask if they want to repeat it. Leaving the room can lead to students asking you to leave regularly!

2 Notes

Ask one student to take notes for the whole group: summarising the main point discussed. Duplicate these notes and pass them round at the next meeting. Improves students' record of discussions and leaves most free to listen and join in.

3 53

Loan the student whose turn it is to present a seminar the book: **53 Interesting things to do in your seminars and tutorials** (details at the end of this section and at the back of this book) and suggest that at least two of the methods are tried out.

4 Problems

Give problems to groups who then solve them and explain their solution to other groups who have had sight of the problem but have not seriously tackled it.

5 Furniture

Rearrange the furniture: try a circle or a horseshoe, syndicate groups, circles or a fishbowl (concentric circles). Suggest the students re-arrange the furniture as they like it, including where you sit and what you sit on. Change the layout half way through and see if it makes any difference.

6   Outsider

Sit outside the seminar circle so that you can hear what is going on, but do not take part except at pre-specified points, e.g. at half-time, at the end.

7   Case study

Get groups to devise case studies for other groups to work on. Discuss solutions/ analyses in the whole class after groups have worked on each other's cases. In sessions longer than one hour students can devise the case study in the session, without any prior warning.

8   Circular questioning

In response to questions, instead of answering yourself, try sending the question back with: "If you were to ask ..... her response to that question, what do you think it would be?" Name a member of the group, a fellow lecturer, a public figure or a key theorist as the person whose answer you are asking the questioner to formulate.

9   Walkabout

Try having a one-to-one tutorial whilst going on a short walk together. It is often easier to talk to someone while you are jointly engaged in a common task.

10   Silent classes

Don't allow talking! All communication must be written down. This encourages careful reflection before "speaking" in writing.

11   Third years

Have third year students give seminars to first years. Train them in the task.

12   Role play discussions

Ask students to take the role of different people such as politicians, or theorists, in a case study or debate. They prepare both content and personal style. Have opposing characters in the role play.

13   Fishbowl with observers

A fishbowl involves having those not directly involved sitting round the outside of a seminar group. You can also have observers responsible for:

a   giving feedback on the contributions of chosen partners in the inner group;

b   making comments on the processes at work in the inner group at selected points;

c   looking for applications, social implications, generalisations etc. according to a brief, and reporting on these at the end.

14   Lecturers' role play

Two or more lecturers discuss a famous debate or controversy in the subject, taking the roles and arguments of the key protagonists. Allow the students to ask questions, as in a T.V. studio debate with an audience.

15   Seminar assessment

Assess students' seminar presentations: not just the content but the process. How clear was the presentation? How well were students' questions elicited and answered? Were follow-up readings and references given?

16   Peer assessment

Have the student group assess their peer's seminar presentation. Either use a pro forma with criteria (as in **15 Seminar Assessment** above), or have a class discussion about what the criteria should be at the start.

17   Audience assessment

Assess participants' contributions to seminars, as well as the presenter's contributions. Did students prepare well? Did they join in constructively? Did they even turn up? You can arrange for this assessment to be done by the students themselves, too: they can be very tough on their colleagues who do not pull their weight or who are obstructive.

18   Reading during seminars

Allow short periods during the seminar for everyone to read a handout or a section from a key text, or even, during two or three hour sessions, to make a quick visit to the library to research a topic. The immediacy of the reading helps students to participate in discussion.

19   Setting

Hold the seminar in the bar, the pub, coffee room, Hall of Residence: somewhere with an atmosphere different to a classroom and more conducive to freer social interaction.

20   Name map

If you don't already know everybody's name, draw a map of the room on an OHP and write everyone's name on it where they are sitting. Display this name map for you and the students to use to address everyone by name.

21   Court of enquiry

Set debates up as formal courts of enquiry. Use formal procedures such as having opposing factions, calling witnesses, cross examining witnesses, making a final ruling, etc.

22   Agenda

Clarify the agenda for the discussion at the start. Display the agenda on the board, refer to it, use it to move on to new topics, change it as the discussion progresses. Ask students to help you to devise the agenda.

23   Roles

Give individual students specific roles to perform in the group: timekeeper, chair, secretary/note-taker, arbitrator/honest broker, process-observer/commentator, summariser, etc.

24   Offerings

At the start of a seminar or tutorial, check out what students have brought with them to the meeting. What have they read? What questions do they have? What would they like to tell others? Be clear what your resources are before you decide how to proceed. (See also **22 Agenda**).

25   Selective reading list

Try setting a very small piece of selected reading which is a minimum for those who are not presenting, or divide reading up between group members with individuals each having responsibility for a small area. This works well because although most courses have reading lists for seminars, while the presenter tends to take this seriously, everyone else tries to get away with doing nothing.

26   Pyramid

Give students a task to work on alone, put them in pairs to discuss what they have done, in fours to draw conclusions, and hold a full group discussion to compare the fours' conclusions. This invariably increases the involvement of low contributors.

27   Buzz

When the discussion gets bogged down, set a brief task or question for pairs to work on before moving on, e.g.: "What do you want to discuss next?", "What conclusions have you drawn so far?", "What questions do you have outstanding?". It is almost impossible for students to stay quiet and it almost always generates new content and energy.

28   Syndicates

In larger groups, set up groups of 4–6 to work in parallel on the same problem, task or question. Circulate round the groups. Then convene a whole group plenary to which the syndicate groups report. This method can be useful for coping with excessively large 'seminar' groups.

29   Group pattern

Build up a pattern (as in organic notes) on the board to represent the structure of ideas developing as the discussion progresses. Encourage students to add points to the pattern. Use it to point out relationships between ideas, areas which have been neglected, similarities etc.

30   Panel

Lecturers form a panel (as in *Gardeners' Question Time* to answer questions from the group. Have some prepared questions in case of stuckness. Students benefit from seeing disagreements and limits of lecturer's knowledge.

31   Line up

Establish a continuum of beliefs or attitudes. e.g.

> *'intelligence is determined:*
> entirely by heredity .... entirely by the environment'

and ask students to line up across the room according to where on the continuum they think they stand. Get them to negotiate with those either side of them to make sure they are in the right place on the continuum in relation to those around them. This guarantees personal involvement and getting off the fence. It can be noisy and sometimes acrimonious!

32   Terrible discussions I have known

Have a discussion of what makes a good seminar discussion. Start by asking students to recall one terrible, and one excellent discussion, and to write down the main features of these discussions. Use a pyramid (see **26**) to share these experiences in pairs, and then draw out general truths in groups of four. Finally pool and discuss those things which seem to make discussions go well or badly. Finish by everyone (including yourself) making personal statements about how they are going to behave in future. e.g. *'I am going to try not to..... and I am going to.....'.*

33   Rounds

A round simply involves everyone in the group, in turn going round the circle, saying something on a particular theme. It might be *"Questions I would like to have answered"*, *"Notions I find difficult"*, *"Something I will take away with me from this discussion"*, *"What I now want to go and work on"*, etc.

34 Circular interviewing

The group sits in a circle and each student in turn interviews the person sitting opposite (either about the topic in general, or about work specially prepared by that student). The interviewing rotates so that both the interviewer and interviewee roles move one place to the left until everyone has both interviewed and been interviewed.

A wider range of ideas for interesting ways to teach in groups can be found in *53 Interesting things to do in your seminars and tutorials* which contains detailed instructions and procedures as well as rationales for teaching methods. The contents of this book are listed below:

STARTING OFF

STUDENT-LED SEMINARS

GROUP WORK

ENCOURAGING STUDENTS TO PARTICIPATE

Information on how to order *53 Interesting things to do in your seminars and tutorials* can be found inside the back cover.

4 Laboratory work

1 Extrapolation

Take a piece of standard equipment or an experiment with which your students are familiar, and make a massive change or disturbance in something which is normally kept the same – a temperature or a parameter as for instance using a diamond-shaped notch at the end of a pipe instead of a circular one in an hydraulics experiment. Require the students to predict the result before carrying out the experiment to confirm their prediction. Alternatively, have small groups of students decide on changes in parameters with which to confront their colleagues in other groups.

2 Sabotage

Present the students with an experiment or apparatus with which they are familiar and invite them surreptitiously to sabotage the experiment so that those who follow will get the wrong results and won't notice that there is anything wrong. They should aim for an error that is as high as possible and should estimate what it should be. They should verify this for themselves subsequently by using the equipment themselves. Award a prize for the best sabotage.

3 Kindergarten

Dream up a competition which calls for good understanding of fundamentals, expressed in as childish a form as the "Great Egg Race". Test fluid mechanics and friction with a bar of soap and a wooden ramp which can be inclined to a varying slope and award a prize to the group who can get their carved soap "boat" furthest across the "pond" from the "launching ramp". Then require the groups to identify what made for the best performance.

4 Deduction

Present students with a complex piece of equipment and possibly with its title and require them to work out for themselves how it is to be used – and then confirm that diagnosis by using it.

5   Instant lab report

Require students to submit their lab report as they leave the lab. This can have a whole range of consequences for how, and how quickly, they go about their lab work, what notes they take as they go along, how closely they listen to your initial briefing, etc.

6   No procedure labs

Instead of designing the entire lab session yourself and providing students with a recipe to follow, simply tell them: *"Measure X/determine the value of Y/ demonstrate the relationship between A and B"*.   Leave all the necessary equipment around. If you give them the brief the week before they can start planning and reading in advance. They will not cover as much ground or execute as elegant an experiment as usual, but they will learn more about experimental design and probably about the concepts as well.

7   Full procedure labs

The opposite of (6) above, to be used when it is practice in using equipment, developing techniques and skills or recording and analysing data which is important. Provide very full instructions, data recording sheets, blank spaces in formulae etc. This can speed student work and it also eases marking. It can also result in students disengaging their brains.

8   Half and half labs

Set half the students the task of designing a laboratory session for the other half to execute, and vice versa. The students should select equipment and write out procedures and brief the other half on the theory underlying the practical work. They should subsequently mark their work. The group on the receiving end should make comments on the experimental design and procedure. Alternatively you can mark the work but the groups get the average mark of the other group. A follow up discussion with both groups may be necessary to avoid bloodshed.

9   Didn't they do badly?

Present a group of students with apparatus and a practical problem for which they will not find it easy to deduce an answer. Alternatively ask the group to execute a procedure in a mild variant of a familiar situation. Arrange the group in a "fishbowl" with an audience of the rest of the class round them, watching. After 15 or 20 minutes planning, and possibly after playing around with the apparatus, call on members from the audience to appraise the ideas and procedures developed and used.

10   Detection

Either show a video of someone carrying out an experiment with unfamiliar equipment, or for an unfamiliar purpose, or give a demonstration yourself in the laboratory. The students, without much consultation, and in small groups, are required to work out what you are doing and why.

11   Invention

Present the students with a "kit" of equipment with which they are reasonably familiar, and challenge them to think of as many different experiments as possible which will use this, or some of this, to demonstrate principles which you select, or to obtain particular results.

12   Error

Give a piece of falsified equipment and require students to find the error and then the source.

13   Notional project

Given an open-ended problem, students:

   a   formulate and defend an hypothesis on the basis of which an experiment would be designed;

b   design an experiment to test the hypothesis.

Students do not carry out the experiment, but predict the outcome.

14   Finish it

Students draft conclusions and suggestions for further work after being shown a piece of equipment (perhaps from postgraduate research or undergraduate project work) and a set of results. A thesis, project report or paper based on the experimental work can be used to help.

15   Follow my leader

Set up an experiment to run for an entire week. Group after group pick it up and carry it on for an hour or so and then leave instructions for the next group. Make it an enquiry for which no-one in the department knows the answer.

16   Teach the teacher

Instruct students to take any experiment with which they are familiar, identify the basic concept which it demonstrates, and change the experiment so that the emphasis is purely on the demonstration of that concept and the learning activity restricted to that. Ask them to submit plans for this experiment. Use the best plans next time!

17   Exploitation

Give students one piece of apparatus with which they are familiar and ask them to design a set of experiments which together cover as many aspects of the taught syllabus as possible. (Similar to **11 Invention**).

18   Twenty questions

Pairs of students are given a new experiment which they carry out. Others then have to find out what was done, why, and what conclusions were reached – but only 20 questions which can be answered 'yes' or 'no' can be asked.

19   The world is our lab

Ask students to find something happening somewhere in the Polytechnic or University where the behaviour demonstrates a principle or phenomenon or finding which they have already learnt in the laboratory. Then ask them to devise an experiment to determine whether the real life situation is accurately predicted by the laboratory experiment.

20   Mutiny

Require students to devise a worthwhile experiment for a piece of equipment in the laboratory which is not normally used for that purpose, carry out the experiment, and demonstrate its usefulness and relevance.

21   Interaction

Given a situation in which there can be three relevant parameters, rather than the traditional one in which one variable is plotted against another to give a graph, require students to design and carry out the least possible number of experiments to determine the interrelationship with these three parameters. They should demonstrate by experiment that they have succeeded.

22   Video

When you have large classes split into multiple groups for demonstrations of techniques, videotape the first demonstration you do and allow subsequent groups to view this video at the start of, and during, their lab sessions instead of you having to repeat the demonstration. Borrow portable video equipment and film it yourself, or ask technicians or students to do it for you. You could even set groups the task of making good videos of demonstrations, and using their products subsequently.

23 Audio instructions

Tape record your verbal instructions for a lab on an ordinary cassette recorder. Make several copies and provide students with several recorders and tapes in the class. Students, alone or in small groups, can listen when they are ready, repeat bits they find tricky, have the tape running while they carry out the tasks, replay it afterwards whilst writing up their report, etc. Audio recordings are cheap and easy compared with video recordings.

24 Poster sessions

Ask students who have been undertaking varied experimental work in parallel to display the outcomes on posters in the laboratory so that other students can see what they have got up to. Many conferences nowadays have poster sessions so that a large audience can gain a quick appreciation of the range of work going on.

5   Assessment

1 Pass the problem

Students in groups of 6–10 are give 6–10 problems or exercises. Student 1 does problem 1 and passes it to student 2 who marks it and solves problem 2, passing this to student 3 who marks problem 2 and so on until everyone has undertaken and marked one problem.

2 Mastery learning

Set a standard (e.g. 80% in a test, or a list of problem types which must all be mastered) and every member of the class must reach this standard before the class proceeds. If the students are put into small groups they will naturally tutor each other through material in order that the whole group can proceed. You will need alternative forms of tests to enable the same material to be assessed at the second or third attempt.

3 Student hand-back

Write full comments on students' work and then hand it back not to the students who wrote it, but to their partner (in pairs). The students, in turn, give each other tutorials on the work, using your notes and comments and marks to give feedback on their partners' strengths and weaknesses.

4 Library search

Set twenty or so library search problems (e.g. *"Find and write down the full reference to two reviews of the book: ...."*). Students work in pairs on the search. Such searches can be done in an hour and marked in class immediately, followed by a discussion of search techniques and tricks. Ask your subject librarian to help set the questions.

5 Book review

Set students the task of reviewing a book, maximum 500 words, instead of othe assessed written work. In seminars have the students read each others' review and discuss the books and their different reviews. Students can also writ summaries or formal abstracts of experiments and research papers.

6 Contracts

Students write themselves contracts for the week and specify what they will do to learn the subject matter for that week (e.g. "I contract to read X and Y and do six practice problems of the form . . ."), and how they will demonstrate that they have fulfilled their contract (e.g. "I will solve any problem of the following kind that a fellow student could set"). Students, in groups, look at each other' contracts to make sure they are not too easy or difficult to achieve, and give advice about sensible changes. At the end of the week the students, in the same groups assess each other in terms of whether their contracts have been fulfilled, on a pass fail basis.

7 DIY

You do the the assignment you have set your students and copy the outcome for students to see and comment on (after their own attempts have been returned).

8 Self assessment sheets

Require all assessed work to be submitted with a self-assessment sheet which requires students to write down: *"What is good about this is . . .", "What is weak about this is . . .", "What I would need to do to to make it better is . . .", "It deserves a mark of . . . because . . .".*

9   Verbal mock exam

Show the students last year's exam paper two thirds of the way through the course so students can see how they are getting on and what they need to work harder on. Go through the 'answers' verbally, in a lecture. Get them to tell you which bits of the course so far they feel they are best/worst at.

10   Seminar presentation

Assess students' seminar presentations, paying particular attention to presentation skills as well as to content. Make your assessment criteria clear and have a discussion of how best to meet them. Allow students to assess the presenter using a pro forma listing the agreed criteria. (see also **Seminars** items **15–17**).

11   Spot test

Spring tests on students which they will not have prepared for: don't count the results, but use them for feedback to the students on what they have learnt and what they have not. Get the students to mark each other's work, using your answer sheet. Award a booby prize (a dead biro ?) to the worst student.

12   Multiple choice questions

Use objective tests to test large numbers of students painlessly and give them feedback. Write the questions on OHP transparencies and display them in class, to avoid having to print anything.

13   Teach test

Teach Test involves setting clear objectives for a week's work (e.g. "By next week you should be able to . . ."). In class the first half of the time is spent with students working through a test of last week's objectives, with the lecturer touring around being helpful: the test is a means to give individual tutorial time to students

LIBRARY
BISHOP BURTON COLLEGE
BEVERLEY HU17 8QG

rather than to assess them. In the second half of the class the next week's objectives are explained and a summary lecture of the topic given. Students prepare for the tests on their own, or with their colleagues, from textbooks. This technique was developed at Trent Polytechnic by Terry Vickers and is used mainly with BTEC courses with clear objectives.

14 Role play essay

Suggest that students take on a role and write for a specific audience. e.g. *"Imagine you are a French journalist working for Le Monde. Write an article for the front page about Britain's attitude towards trade in agricultural produce within the EEC in the context of recent incidents involving French farmers"* or *"Advise Weybridge Electrical, for whom you are a consultant, on the suitability of the circuit designs below, given the performance specifications listed"*. Role play essays can be very helpful because asking students to write essays for you, when you know more than they do about what they are writing, can cause problems of sorting out who the real audience is.

15 Assessing accuracy in practical work

In practicals concerned with establishing constants and standard values, allocate marks to students according to how accurate their results are. You can make this estimated from the class mean and standard deviation. Allocating marks according to accuracy increases students' care in their work.

16 Assessing group work

You can allocate everyone in a group which has carried out a joint piece of work the same grade, but this sometimes seems unfair. Instead, either:

a   Allocate a total sum of marks to be divided by the group as they see fit.

b   Get the group members to assess each other's contributions using a set of agreed criteria, e.g. contributions to writing up, to analysis of data, to original ideas, to leading the group etc. For each criterion the student gets the group grade if he/she has made what is judged to be a full contribution, but loses marks for each of the criteria on which a less than full contribution has been made.

17   Student requests for feedback

Ask students, when they submit work for assessment, what it is about the work which they would really like feedback on. This helps you to focus your written comments and helps to ensure that they read what you write!

18   Diaries and log books

Ask students to keep logs of their work: their reading, practical work, notes, discussions, quiet reflections etc and submit this for assessment or feedback. You would be looking for the quality of their reflections and analyses and for the breadth of their work.

19   Staff marking exercise

Type up a piece of student work and get all your colleagues to mark it: commenting and allocating a mark or grade. Then meet and discuss your views and marks. Try to arrive at a set of criteria which explain how you have marked the work. Write these out so that students can see what they are supposed to be aiming for. This kind of exercise can be very important on team-taught courses.

20   Student marking exercise

As **19**, but the students mark the piece of work and try to arrive at shared criteria. Use pyramids as a discussion technique (see **Seminars** item **26**). You can then come in and tell them what happened when the lecturers marked the same piece of work (if you dare!). To conclude, ask the students to set themselves directions: *"Next time I do a piece of work like this I am going to try to . . ."*.

21   Interpretation of evidence

Give students the results of an experiment, some interview transcripts, an extract from census data, the financial report of a company etc and ask them to interpret the evidence. Add data interpretation to conventional essay titles e.g. *"What light is thrown on Triesman's model of selective attention by the following experimental results . . . ?"*

22   Design

Set your students a design task, e.g. *"Design an experiment (or a study of evidence or literature) to test the hypothesis that . . ."* (and fill in a suitable hypothesis for your subject). Design tasks are common in Architecture and Engineering but they can also be used in most other subjects.

23   Mock exam

Get the students to sit last year's exam half way through the course so that they can see what they know and what they don't. (see also **9 Verbal Mock Exam**).

24   Two-stage assignment

Have students submit a full draft which you mark (allocating 30% of the marks) and give feedback on how to improve the work for final submission. This is much closer to the normal development process of a journal article or research report.

25   Crit

The crit is an assessment in which a student's plans and other work are displayed in an exhibition and a group of staff and students listen to an explanation of the exhibition and then ask questions. The crit is a well known assessment method in architecture but this format can also be used for the outcomes of project work in other subject areas.

A wider range of assessment methods, together with detailed rationales and explanations, can be found in: *53 Interesting ways to assess your students*, the contents of which are listed below:

ESSAYS

1   Standard essay
2   Role play essay
3   Structured essay
4   Interpretation of evidence
5   Design
6   Note-form essays
7   Hypothesis formation

OBJECTIVE TESTS

8   Right/wrong
9   Short answer
10   Completion
11   True/false
12   Matching
13   Multiple choice
14   Multiple completion
15   Assertion/reason
16   Best answer

ALTERNATIVE EXAMS

17   Seen exam
18   168-Hour exam
19   Revealed exam questions
20   Open book exam
21   'Doing it' exam

COMPUTER BASED ASSESSMENT

22   Computer marking
23   Computer generated test papers
24   Computer generated problems
25   Computer feedback to students
26   Computer based Keller plan
27   Assessed computer simulations
28   Computer marked practicals

ASSESSING PRACTICAL AND PROJECT WORK

29   Viva
30   Crits
31   Observation
      Assessing group project work
32   Shared group grade
33   Peer assessment of contribution to group
34   Second marker's sheet
35   Exhibition
36   Diaries and log books
37   Project exam
38   The instant lab report
39   Laboratory notes

CRITERIA

40   Criteria for students
41   Project criteria
42   Negotiating criteria
43   Marking schemes
44   Staff marking exercise
45   Profiles
46   Hidden criteria
47   Criterion referenced assessment
48   Pass/fail

FEEDBACK TO STUDENTS

49   Teach-test
50   SAQ's
51   Feedback classroom
52   Student requests for feedback
53   Feedback checklists

Information on ordering *53 Interesting ways to assess your students* can be found inside the back cover.

5 Independent study

1. Reading week
2. Learning contracts
3. Video
4. Handbook
5. Poem
6. Student review
7. Newspapers
8. Essay co-operation
9. Reading guide
10. When the book is out . . .
11. Week-long projects
12. Fieldwork/visit
13. Out of hours
14. Syndicates
15. Research proposals
16. Study guide
17. Lab/practical/fieldwork guide
18. Self help group
19. Peer viva
20. Diary
21. Student games, case studies, simulations and role plays
22. Textbook
23. Open university
24. Video/audiotape
25. Letters
26. Marketplace
27. What advice will I give?
28. Reading deals
29. Broadening horizons
30. Merger
31. Top ten
32. Reciprocal supervision
33. How can I help you?
34. Exhibition guide
35. Intermediate deadline
36. Reciprocal reading list
37. TV presentation

1   Reading week

Cancel classes, but give plenty of help to students to plan the way they will spend their time. In particular, help them to plan their reading, perhaps using contracts (see **2**, below).

2   Learning contracts

Ask each student to draw up a learning contract (*'I contract to learn ......'*) written in a way which operationalises a general intention through specific courses of action which are verifiable by the group with whom the student draws up the contract. Students get their contract signed by their group, after negotiation about its content. Students meet a week later to discuss what they managed to achieve in relation to their learning contract.

3   Video

Students make a video of the week in a way which would be genuinely helpful to the students doing that week next year.

4   Handbook

As (3) but students produce a handbook or manual to the week, with notes, advice, etc., for next year's students.

5   Poem

Ask students to write a poem about their subject, their experience of the Polytechnic or University, as a course review, or on a topic of their choice, and display these (anonymously if necessary) on the walls of the next class.

6   Student review

Students undertake a course review with the aim of informing the way the rest of the course operates. Tell them you will try to respond to whatever they suggest but that they must have convincing evidence to back up their suggestions.

7   Newspapers

Set students the task of collecting recent items from the press about selected topics on the course. Share and discuss these press items in seminars, or in an impromptu lecture.

8   Essay co-operation

Allow students to form groups of up to four to work on problem sheets or essay questions. Agree to give the same mark to each individual in the group.

9   Reading guide

Instead of a reading list, give some advice about the recommended sources, e.g. *"readable but out of date"*, *"dull but thorough"*, *"Better on X than on Y"*, *"Useful as an alternative to Z"*. Collect advice from students to help you.

10   When the book is out . . .

Students regularly face the problem of finding that the recommended text is out of the library when it is needed. In seminars, brainstorm ideas for coping with this problem (e.g. find book reviews, use the Encyclopaedia of . . ., find another book by the same author, find a journal article by the same author etc). Choose a book you know is out (you have it out yourself !) and ask all students to go straight to the library to try out one of the suggested solutions which they have never tried before. Then discuss what transpired.

11   Week-long projects

Set a task which involves students in a week's independent work (about 8-10 hours). Cancel classes for a week and use class time the following week to summarise the outcomes.

12   Fieldwork/visit

Arrange an activity, trip, visit or piece of fieldwork for those students who don't normally go outside the Polytechnic or University.

13   Out of hours

People work best at different times of the day. Suggest students try something completely new, like working before 8 in the morning, to see how it feels. Discuss these experiments in class.

14   Syndicates

Set syndicate groups questions. Groups go to the library, etc. in search of answers, and report back at the end of the week at special group presentation where the lecturer clears up any gaps or misapprehensions.

15   Research proposals

Student groups formulate research proposals and present these to a panel of academics, students and members of the community.

16   Study guide

Write down: *"What I want you to learn this week is . . . . You can find out about it here . . . . and here . . . . Here are some questions for you to check whether you have done enough work .... These are the kind of exam questions asked on this topic .... Here are my own summary notes as an outline .... This is what we will be discussing in class"*. Don't lecture, just hand your guide to students and have a discussion at the end of the week.

17   Lab/practical/fieldwork guide

As for (**16**), but it provides full notes to support practical work which requires little or no supervision and which might be able to be set up on an open access basis for students to complete in any one of a number of sessions.

18   Self help group

Organise students into self help groups. In class, set groups up to discuss what they might be able to do to support each other in their learning, and how and when the group should meet. Agree a time to reconvene to discuss progress, ways of working which the groups have found productive etc.

19   Peer viva

Arrange students into pairs and give them equal time to have vivas with each other about their essay/project/design, taking turns to be 'examiner' and 'student'.

20   Diary

Show students how to keep a diary about their learning, to record their reflections, ideas, problems which need sorting etc. Put time aside in class for students to share and discuss what they have written in their diaries.

21 Student games, case studies, simulations and role plays

It can be valuable to bring some of the real world into the classroom by running games, simulations or role plays which dramatise and make personal the issues and problems being tackled on the course. Devising material for such exercises can be time consuming, so ask students to do it for you, and get them to run the sessions. Act as a consultant to the students whilst they are formulating their exercises.

22 Textbook

At the start of your lecture say: *"This is all in your textbook. Here are some questions that you need to be able to answer. Study pages X–Y until you can answer them. I'll pick up any outstanding queries in the seminars."* Ask the students how it went and what other help they might welcome next time you set them to learn on their own.

23 Open University

Check out if any of your subject is dealt with in Open University course units (or other open learning material) and suggest students work exclusively from this material for that topic.

24 Video/audio tape

Arrange to record broadcast programmes (or check if what you want is in the library already). Put the videotape or audio tape in the library. Set questions for students to answer from the video or audio tape and expect them to study the tape in the library on their own.

25   Letters

Ask students to write to a professional concerned with their subject about some practical aspect of their work. Help them with names and addresses and likely topics. Share replies in seminars.

26   Marketplace

Get students to announce: *"I would like someone to explain to me about ..."* and then ask who would be prepared to try to explain these things in small groups or one-to-one. Help students to form spontaneous peer teaching groups to deal with these queries. Tour the groups helping with difficulties. Reconvene after 10 or 15 minutes and have another round of announcements.

27   What advice will I give?

Some students prefer to be told what to do rather than try to be independent. Try the line: *"If I were to advise you on this, what kinds of things would I say?"* Students can often generate their own advice!

28   Reading deals

Students in pairs or threes divide up the reading list and agree to share out the work, taking notes which can be copied and passed round, and briefing each other on what they have read.

29   Broadening horizons

Set a project involving writing a foreign policy/ health policy/ nuclear power policy/ broadcasting policy/ science policy (choose according to subject area) for a country of the students' choice.

30   Merger

Merge 1st, 2nd, 3rd years, full time and part time students, degree and BTEC students, in a joint problem-solving task and break down normal barriers and suspicions.

31   Top ten

You and your colleagues each write out a list of your all time top ten books, with notes on the reasons for your choice, and hand out this list or pin it up on the notice board. Or hold lunchtime seminars in which you and your colleagues explain their personal top tens. This can inspire students to widen their reading and also reveals something of the human being in teachers.

32   Reciprocal supervision

In project and dissertation supervision, ask your student to tell you how she thinks you are getting on as a supervisor.

33   How can I help you?

Ask this early on in any project or dissertation supervision role and keep asking it at every meeting.

34   Exhibition guide

Select a public exhibition related to your course (an equipment exhibition, town planning exhibition, art exhibition, museum exhibition, etc.) and write a brief guide so that students can go there independently and gain from the experience.

35 Intermediate deadline

Have an intermediate deadline during a longer-running project or dissertation. Have students who are working independently come together and show each other the progress they are making. Give feedback which students can use to improve their project.

36 Reciprocal reading list

Ask the student whose project or dissertation work you are supervising: *"And what would you like me to read?"*

37 TV presentation

Ask student groups who are completing a group project to present the project report to camera. The whole class can then watch the videos which groups have made. This is useful for students who will have to learn to use the media effectively, and it also improves the quality and conciseness of presentations

6   Language teaching

The ideas in this section assume that French is being taught, but they are appropriate for other languages, including English for EFL or ESL teaching. Some of these ideas would also work well as communication skill exercises for science, technology and business students.

1   Interpreter

"Interpreter" involves groups of 3, with three roles rotating. One person plays the role of someone who speaks only English; one person plays the role of someone who speaks only French; one person plays the role of interpreter and translates one to the other as quickly as possible.

2   Voice over

Play a video without the sound. Students in turn provide a French commentary as the video is playing.

3   Breaking in

The group sits in a circle. Two people are chosen to go into the centre and start speaking in French. Other individuals join in the conversation when they see an opening. As each individual goes into the centre, the one who's been there longer leaves, so that there are always just two people in the centre.

4   Confrontation

Students in pairs role play confronting situations such as:

a   teacher and pupil;

b   manager and assistant;

c   boss and secretary;

d   policeman and suspect or customs officer and tourist;

e   shop assistant and customer.

5   Relay debate

Each person in the group is allocated a number. One member of the group initiates, in French, a debate on a contemporary issue. After a reasonable time (say 60–90 seconds) the teacher signals for a change of speaker at which point the person speaking calls out a number who will be the next person to speak. This person first of all summarises the comments of the previous speaker and then continues the debate until the next time signal when the operation is repeated.

6   Directions

Each student writes directions in French for getting from the classroom to somewhere else on the campus but without saying what the destination is. Students then give their set of instructions to a partner who follows them and reports back, in French, on where s/he ends up.

7   Song

Students write French words to a well-known English song, e.g. *"God save the Queen"*, or *"On Ilkley Moor bah't 'at"*.   The class sings one or more of the versions.

8   Chanson

Reverse of (7) above where students write an English version of a well-known French song, e.g. *"La Marseillaise"*, or *"Alouette"*.

9   Instructions

Students write French instructions for using a hair dryer, modern typewriter, etc. Or the teacher brings an obscure piece of equipment into the classroom and gets the students to write imaginary instructions for it.

10   Prospectus

Students write a description of their course in French for inclusion in an alternative prospectus.

11   Interview

Students interview each other in pairs in French on why they're on the course, time spent abroad etc. The interviewer reports back in French to the rest of the group:

   a   in a two minute verbal report, or

   b   a 500 word written report, on what they have discovered about their partner.

12   Visitor

Students work in pairs, imagining that their partner is a French visitor to the polytechnic or University. One takes the other round, pointing out anything of interest and explaining and describing things in French.

13   Video

Students produce a 10 minute current affairs video in French for use in local schools.

14   Recipe

Students write recipes and instructions in French for a set meal for four. Then cook it! A collection of such recipes can be produced as a short recipe book.

15   Lexicon

Play a French version of the English game "Lexicon" with ab initio students.

16   Thank you letter

Students write two "thank you" letters to speakers at their recent (imaginary) conference on the employment of modern languages graduates in the EEC:

a   one to a speaker who gave a very successful presentation,

b   and one to a speaker who was a flop.

17   Crossword

Collect the quick crossword blank from a *Guardian* and collect the solution from the following day's edition. Using the solutions as your base, produce a set of clues in French and ask students to complete the crossword in English.

18   In the manner of the adverb

The following game is played entirely in French. One person volunteers to leave the room temporarily while the others choose an adverb. The volunteer returns and tries to guess the chosen word by asking specific people in the group to mime certain actions, e.g. *"Brush your hair 'in the manner of the adverb'"*. When the volunteer has guessed the adverb by observing a few of these actions, another volunteer leaves the room and a new adverb is chosen.

19   Brief

In French, students brief the Mayoress of Toulouse, prior to her visit to the Council House as guest of the Council, on three big issues which are exercising the minds of local women today.

20   News review

In French, students write a newspaper report, or a 60 second TV report, on one of the following:

    a   the education reform bill going through Parliament in early 1988;

    b   the Government's privatisation programme for 1988;

    c   the introduction of the "Poll Tax".

21   Campus novel

In French, students draft the outline of a campus novel based on their experience of studying.   The draft should include at least three of the following:

    a   a radical student group;

    b   a much resented use of power;

    c   an 'equal opportunities' incident;

    d   unanticipated consequences of the institution's 'inclement weather procedure';

    e   a malign influence.

7 Helping students to learn effectively

1 Anxieties

Ask students to each write down three anxieties they have about studying. (e.g. *"I'm very apprehensive about the size of the reading list"*, *"All my course work deadlines are in the same week"*.) In groups, get students to pool these anxieties into a comprehensive list on the board. Discuss ways of reducing anxieties and overcoming problems for each item on the list.

2 Different types of lecture

Students often treat all lectures as if they were the same. Get individual students to try to identify two lecturers who are very different. Pool these types and pull together a list of different types of lecture. Discuss how you can learn most effectively in these different types of lecture (e.g. by reading before/after, by taking full notes, by only noting references, by having the textbook on your knees during the lecture etc).

3 Mottoes

After discussing problems with studying on your course (perhaps as in 1 above) get students to generate mottoes (like *"Do it NOW"*, *"Think positive"*, *"Take a bus and read a book"*) which address these problems. Display these mottoes on the board.

4 Concentrating

Concentration cannot be achieved at will, but you can learn how to get into situations where you find yourself concentrating. Get students to think of specific instances when they were concentrating or not concentrating, and to explain these situations to each other in groups of four. The groups then generate advice in the form *"We find that we are concentrating when . . . ."* and *"We find that we lose concentration when . . . ."* Pool and display this advice.

5   Understanding and remembering

Students often try to memorise material which needs to be understood. List a whole range of topics, facts and concepts in your subject area and get students to discuss, in small groups, which require to be understood and explained and which only need to be remembered.

6   The next five minutes

Students are not always effective at using whatever time periods become available to them to study. Ask students to write down, in detail, what they could do if, magically, you were able to give them an extra 5 minutes, 30 minutes, one hour and three hours before the end of the class. Get students to compare with each other what they have written down. Then ask them to write down a series of current study tasks which could realistically be completed in these time slots.

7   This term

Get students to draw up a schedule for the remainder of the term, semester or year. Get them to put into this schedule every deadline for course work, exams, preparation for field work, laboratory reports, revision, etc. Then ask them to work backwards from these deadlines to when they need to start all these study tasks. After students have seen each other's plans, each student should complete the sentence: *"One thing I am going to do to organise my studying is . . . ."*

8   Negative advice

Ask a group to call out all the advice they can think of for how to fail the course. Write these on the board. Then ask them to work in small groups to turn this negative advice into sensible positive advice for how to pass the course easily. Students find it much easier to start with how to fail!

9   Skills review

After a discussion of what it takes to do well on the course, or to learn from lectures, or to write essays (see for example item **8** above) get students to write down:

a   *'Things I know how to do, things that I'm good at'*

b   *'Things I am working on and could get better at'*

c   *'Things I need to start working on if I am going to do better'*

Get students to share what they have written down about what they need to work on and get better at: they may be able to help each other!

10   Project stages

Project work, in whatever discipline, has a characteristic sequence of stages. For a technological problem this might be:

a   define problem

b   generate possible solutions

c   collect and organise information about possible solutions

d   evaluate alternative solutions

e   state selected solution

f   plan project to implement solution

g   detail design work

h   production of hardware

i   laboratory testing of hardware

j   on-site testing of hardware

k   evaluation of changed situation

Get your students to generate as detailed a list as possible of the stages of the project work they are involved in, and display and discuss alternative lists.

11 Reading lists

Ask your students to all look at your reading list(s). Ask them to discuss how they make their choices about what to read, and how much. Finish with each student making a statement about something new they will do about choosing what to read and when to stop.

12 SQ3R

SQ3R stands for Survey, Question, Read, Recall, Review. It is a structured reading technique which can be very powerful for students who find that they are reading without purpose or learning (full descriptions are available in most 'How to Study' books). Explain the technique and ask every student to tackle one chapter or article using this technique before the next class session, and then discuss how it went.

13 Reading flexibly

Students read all sorts of different types of material (from the Daily Mirror to computer manuals and philosophy essays) and for all sorts of different purposes (e.g. for entertainment, to be able to do something, to prepare for participating in a discussion). Despite this variation they often don't vary their reading habits much. Get them to list all the different types of material they read, and what they read it for, and then get them to generate advice about an appropriate way of reading for that purpose. Write all this up on the board.

14 Why take notes?

Many students take notes in the same way from every lecture. Tell one third of the students, before a lecture, that you will give them a multiple choice test of facts at the end. Tell a third that you will ask them to write a summary of the lecture. And tell a third that you will expect them to discuss the lecture in a discussion group. Don't let the students know what you have told the others. After the lecture, let students see each other's notes (they ought to be very different!) and discuss the way note taking should vary with the purpose of the task.

15   Listening and sharing

Many students are too busy taking notes to be able to think about what is being said in a lecture. Arrange for pairs of students to do a deal with each other: one will take full notes on the first half of your lecture and copy them for the other one afterwards and listen in the second half, and the other will listen and then take notes in the second half. Let them know when to swop over. The note taker will probably be very thorough and take good notes and the listener will see what it is like to be able to listen carefully. Discuss the experience: students may want to repeat it!

16   Swop

Take time out during lectures to allow students to swop notes and see what others have noted down, and then add to their own notes.

17   Marking exercise

Type up an essay which gained a moderate-to-poor grade and give a copy to every student in the class. Ask them to mark it: both commenting and grading. Discuss the criteria which the students use and lead into a discussion of what makes a good essay. (This can also be done with a lab report or project report).

18   Explaining

Many of the important features of a good written explanation can be found in instructions to carry out a simple task. Ask students to start writing a set of

77

LIBRARY
BISHOP BURTON COLLEGE
BEVERLEY HU17 8QG

instructions for a visitor to get to your class from the nearest main railway station. After five minutes allow students in threes to help each other. Then share the instructions which have been written and draw out some of the successful and unsuccessful features which would characterise any good instructions.

19   File card essays

This helps students to create essays out of separate bits of information. Every student should have taken notes for the essay they are writing, or have annotated texts with them. Ask them to take a file card and write on it, in one sentence, what one section of notes is saying (or what one section of a text is saying). They carry on creating file cards until they have a pile of them and their notes have been summarised. Students then spread the file cards out in front of them and try to sort them into some kind of sensible order. Not all will fit and some may be repeats and need to be discarded or even redrafted. Allow students to see each other's attempt at a complete "essay" on file cards. Discuss the kinds of structures students have created.

20   Class contract

Discuss those things which happen in class which obstruct learning (e.g. people arriving late, chatting, not preparing, pursuing fruitless lines of questioning relentlessly) and write these up on the board. Then suggest that individuals could make a contract with the class by agreeing, in writing, not to do any of these things. Try to make the statements in the contract as positive as possible. (e.g. *"I agree to turn up on time"*).

21   Induction

Run a brief induction programme to next year's course so that students understand the skills and knowledge which will be called upon. Use students from next year's course to help you.

22   Model

Ask students to draw, sculpt, model, paint, or build a picture of the course as they see it. Join in yourself. View and discuss the images which emerge.

23   Bring a friend

Ask students to bring a friend along from outside the Polytechnic. At the end of a day, ask the friends for their views about what is going on. Students can have a lot of their "taken for granted" perceptions about how to learn effectively exposed in this way.

A wide range of classroom exercises designed to help your students to study
effectively, together with full instructions and all the necessary materials and
handouts, can be found in *53 Interesting ways of helping your students to study*
the contents of which are listed below.

Information about ordering *53 Interesting ways of helping your students to study* can be found inside the back cover.

8 Communication skills

The ideas in this section were developed for science students but most are applicable to other subject areas.

1 Oral exams

To help students prepare for oral exams form them into groups of four. Ask them to generate the kind of questions they think they might be asked in an oral exam. One of each group then leaves the room while the others prepare to examine them. They can re-arrange furniture and decide who is going to ask which questions. The fourth student, who has left, then returns to be examined by the other three. The 'examining panel' can grade the 'candidate'. What went well and badly can be discussed and then the other three students, in turn, have their chance to be examined.

2 Interview skills

As for oral exams (1 above) with groups discussing what sort of questions an employer would ask, and taking it in turns to 'interview' each other.

3 Telephone skills

Ask students to imagine that they have to train recruits to a busy office in telephone skills. Ask them to draw up guidelines highlighting the likely problems of effective telephone communication and some ways to overcome these problems. This exercise can be useful as an alternative to the usual role play exercises which students can dislike.

4 Presentation skills

Ask each student to prepare a 15 minute presentation on a topic of interest outside their area of study. Agree a clear set of criteria for assessing the presentations, and have the students themselves assess each presentation, using the agreed checklist. The checklist could include: room layout, voice, content, structure, notes, handouts, timing, eye contact, visual aids, answering questions, relationship with audience.

5   Overhead projector

Most student seminar presentations would be improved by the effective use of the OHP. Demonstrate its use (or ask a visual aids specialist to do this for you) including as many ideas as possible: revealing material gradually, overlays, lettering sizes, enlarged typescript and graphics etc. Then ask each student to prepare one OHP transparency to display some point or bit of information. Discuss the effectiveness of each transparency in turn.

6   Arranging data in tables

Photocopy the results section of a journal article where data is not presented in tabular form (but would benefit from a table) or where a table is poorly and confusingly laid out, and ask students to lay out the data in a clear table. Look at the best tables which are produced and derive general principles for table design.

7   Presenting information

Ask students to take the data in the table below and to present it visually in an effective way on a poster on the wall. Students could use histograms, graphs, pictograms, use different scales, colour and so on. Everyone then tours the posters and discusses which methods are effective, which are misleading and where the pitfalls lie.

Unemployment in the UK
(in thousands)

1982	1983	1984	1985	1986	1987
2,917	3,105	3,160	3,271	3,408	3,297

8   Operating instructions

Ask students to each select a piece of laboratory equipment and to write operating instructions. They then take it in turns to operate the chosen equipment using only the instructions, and discuss problems and ways to improve the instructions. The session concludes with a set of general principles for writing operating instructions.

9   Abstracts

Choose an article with an excellent abstract and copy the article for your class. Ask students to identify the main features of the abstract, in relation to the content of the article, which make it good. When you have identified general principles, give them copies of articles with the abstract removed and ask them to write an abstract. Then compare the students' abstracts with the author's.

10   Scientific papers

Borrow a set of journals containing scientific papers. Ask students to look at them and to identify the main features and characteristics of scientific papers. Pull together a list of the common features, especially the main section headings and descriptions of the functions of these, and notes on writing style.

11   Rotten reports

Take an extremely poor student lab report (preferably an amusingly awful one) and copy it. Ask students to rewrite it so that it is much better. If they feel information is missing they can ask you for it, but they must know what they are looking for. Compare the reports which students produce and draw up a list of do's and don't's about lab report writing.

12   Plural quiz

Ask students what the plural is of: formula, bacillus, nucleus, appendix, focus, locus, hyperbola, parabola, index, matrix, maximum, bronchus, spectrum, virus, genus, analysis, axis, helix; and what is the singular of: media, bacteria, phenomena, data, criteria, vertebrae, antennae, larvae.

13 Unscientific writing

Popular psuedo-scientific literature provides a useful resource for exploring how language can improperly exploit and massage evidence. Take a passage of Erich von Daniken's *Chariots of the Gods?* and ask students to identify words and phrases which are intended to persuade the reader that evidence is significant. Try to identify as many characteristics of his style as possible. Go on to discuss whether this means that all scientific writing should be dull.

14 The popularisation of science

Ask students to identify, in the popular press, stories based on scientific evidence. Track down the original source (a journal article or conference paper perhaps) and compare the two and discuss the differences.

15 Not only books

Devise a series of library search question which require students to use all the audio-visual equipment in the library: microfiche and microfilm readers, video, audio, slide viewers etc, and also a selection of non-book sources. Get your subject librarian to help. Send teams of students off on the search and come back for a discussion about non-book sources and the equipment involved.

16 Science and society

Encourage students to see the implications of scientific theory for society. Take a powerful scientific notion (e.g. Darwin's theory of natural selection) from the students' subject area and set up a hypothesis that the theory can equally be applied to aspects of human society. Set up groups of students to test the application of the theory to: transport, racism, private enterprise, languages, political parties, education or sport. Ask each group to report back with a brief statement. Watch out for illogical reasoning, deterministic thinking etc.

A collection of communication skill exercises, complete with full instructions and extensive materials, examples and handouts, can be found in *53 Interesting communication exercises for science students*. The contents of this book are listed below:

COMMUNICATION THEORY

1   Communication models
2   Communication barriers
3   Defining communication
4   Different types of communication
5   Body language

THINKING ABOUT SCIENCE

6   Zen and the art of scientific investigation
7   Scientific method: follow the chart
8   Jumping to conclusions
9   Science and society
10   Scientific debate
11   Definitions of science

STUDY SKILLS

12   So I'll give you the time now
13   Essay writing
14   Reading a scientific article
15   Understanding equipment

USING A LIBRARY

16   Not only books I
17   Not only books II
18   Paper-chase

THE LANGUAGE OF SCIENCE

19   Objectivity
20   Writing for an audience
21   The popularisation of science
22   The bermuda triangle
23   Exciting or exploiting?
24   Science on television

TECHNICAL WRITING

25   What's the difference between . . . ?
26   What's the plural of . . . ?
27   A complex problem for copper!

Information concerning how to order *53 Interesting communication exercises for science students* can be found inside the back cover.

9 Evaluating for change

1   Problems self-check list

List every possible problem with your teaching you can think of (such as student attendance, students missing the point of questions, over-preparation for lectures, student lack of participation in seminars). Alongside the list draw up three columns labelled : *"Often a problem for me"*, *"Sometimes a problem for me"*, *"Not a problem for me"*. Run through the list and identify where you think you need to work on your teaching. This exercise is best done co-operatively with colleagues and discussed.

2   Teaching file

Open a file into which you put every piece of evidence you come across about the quality of your course (including notes you make yourself, jottings of comments overheard etc). Go through this file at the end of the course.

3   Understanding student experience

Conventional questionnaires often do not tap important aspects of students' experience. Use open-ended questions and questions which give students permission to talk about wider issues such as their overall interest in continuing to study the subject.

4   Alternatives

Ask students to comment on alternatives to the way you run your course, e.g. instead of asking about details on lecturing technique, ask whether lectures are appropriate at all or whether they would have preferred a project based course.

5   Video

Use video to provide playback of a teaching session. You don't need a fancy production: a static camera without anyone operating it is usually quite enough

 LIBRARY
BISHOP BURTON COLLEGE
BEVERLEY HU17 8QG

for your own purposes. Just watch it on your own or ask an experienced teacher to watch it with you. Then watch part of it with students and get their reactions.

6   Appraisal process

Have a respected and trusted colleague sit in on your teaching for the express purpose of giving you feedback. Afterwards the procedure should be:

a   you comment and make observations before your appraiser does;

b   good points are dealt with before bad points;

c   all comments should be backed up by evidence: how do you know?

d   all negative points should be followed by ideas for improving them;

e   the process should be concluded by an agreement about what action could be taken.

7   Mentors

Arrange to have another person with whom to discuss teaching issues on a regular basis. This method is usually used formally with inexperienced or new teachers but much value can be gained from mentorship with two experienced staff listening to and helping each other. It often works best when you don't know the person too well.

8   One issue meetings

Arrange departmental or course team meetings with only one issue on the agenda, namely a teaching issue of common concern. Collect more than anecdotal evidence to inform this meeting.

9   Diaries

Use a diary to record personal feelings, reflections, observations about your teaching etc as near to the time of the events as possible. Read through your diary at the end of the week. Discuss your diary with someone else who is also keeping a reflective diary. A useful way to start is: *"Dear Diary, this morning I . . . ."*

10 Evaluation swops

Agree with another lecturer (perhaps from a different department) to evaluate each other's courses and teaching. Give each other a completely free hand and meet to discuss what you discover.

11 Outsider evaluation

Use an outsider, an "honest broker", to evaluate your course for you and report confidentially to you.

12 Team teaching

Work co-operatively in class with another lecturer to see what each other get up to, and to get peer feedback on teaching.

13 Learning groups

Form an informal self-help or "special interest" group with limited life expectancy to discuss and solve a problem on a particular teaching issue (e.g. poor essay writing skills exhibited by students, excessively time-consuming marking, working with large seminar classes). The purpose is not to report to others or to link into a committee structure, but to solve a shared problem. The group then dissolves.

14 "What's on top?"

At the start of meetings held for other purposes (such as Departmental Boards or course team meetings) have an open discussion of teaching issues of immediate concern for a limited fixed period (e.g. 15 minutes). The issues should concern teaching and should have been triggered by immediate events (e.g. *"This morning nearly half my class arrived late. Do others have that problem?"*). Put *"What's on top?"* on the agenda for every meeting.

15 The real, real reason I'm not a better teacher . . .

Complete the sentence: *"The real, real reason I am not a better teacher is . . . "* in order to identify the extent to which aspects such as "ability", "opportunity" and "motivation" stop you becoming a better teacher.

16 Soliloquy

Talk into a tape-recorder about your teaching – speak or be silent as you like, in any way you like, for the length of the tape (at least 30 minutes). Listen to it by yourself or with another. Stop the tape whenever you want to comment or think.

17 Instant questionnaire

At the end of a class, write up on the board (or OHP) six statements about students' experience of the class, e.g:

1.   *"I still don't understand Blogg's technique"*
2.   *"I felt I could have understood Y in half the time"*

Students write down the statement numbers, and next to them a rating according to whether they agree with the statement:

A = strongly agree
B = agree
C = unsure
D = disagree
E = strongly disagree

Students hand their pieces of paper in as they leave. In this way you can get instant feedback without typing and printing questionnaires.

18   Letters

Ask your students to write you a letter about their experience of your course so far: *"Dear Dr. Smith, I have found the course so far...."* Students are often more reasonable and thoughtful in letters and find it an easier format in which to express personal feelings.

19   Vox pop

Tour round your Department with a portable video camera asking every student you bump into the same set of questions e.g. *"How do you like studying here?"*, *"What do you like about your courses?"*, *"If you had the power to introduce one change, what would it be?"* Show the video in the coffee lounge or at the next course team meeting.

20   Student vox pop

Ask your students to make a short video as in **19** above.

21   Student-designed questionnaires

Ask your students to design the questionnaire you use to evaluate your course.

22   Equal opportunities audit

Select one or more equal opportunities issues (e.g. sexism, ageism) and review all aspects of your course, with your students' help: the timetable, balance of students, essay titles, language used in discussions etc. Look for ways in which equal opportunities are supported or thwarted. Discuss what moves you could make to further the cause of equal opportunities.

23   Bring a friend

Ask a friend from outside the Polytechnic and academic life to join your teaching for a day, and learn from their outsider's perspective about how the whole thing appears.

24   What happened last time

Show students the feedback from your evaluation of the course last time you ran it. Explain what you are changing and what you are not. Ask them what they think.

A wide range of self-appraisal methods, together with student feedback questionnaires and ways of preparing for appraisal interviews, can be found in *53 Interesting ways to appraise your teaching*. The contents of this book are listed below.

APPRAISAL THROUGH QUESTIONNAIRES

SOURCES OF APPRAISAL EVIDENCE

APPRAISAL USING VIDEO AND AUDIO RECORDINGS

APPRAISAL THROUGH STUDENT FEEDBACK DISCUSSIONS

APPRAISAL WITH HELP FROM COLLEAGUES

OVERALL STRATEGIES FOR COLLECTING EVIDENCE

APPRAISAL INTERVIEWS

Information concerning how to order *53 Interesting ways to appraise your teaching* can be found inside the back cover.

10 Giving students more control

1   Assessment choice

Ask students to devise an appropriate assessment task with which to assess their own learning of the topic in hand. You then set them their own task. Or get five groups each to devise a task or question and offer students the choice of any of the five except the one their own group set.

2   Plan the week

Several weeks in advance put time aside for the students to plan the whole of a week, given the syllabus and past exam papers, assessment regulations or other constraints. They must give you a detailed brief for whatever they want you to do. You can add extra constraints: for example you might wish not to lecture, or to specify a maximum amount of your time which is available.

3   Quiz

Divide the students into two teams. The teams elect a panel of four and devise fiendish (but fair) questions about the course covered so far. Nominate two judges who vet the questions and throw out unfair ones, chair the quiz and select questions to ask, judge whether questions have been answered fairly and keep the score. Tape record a popular radio quiz programme for students to copy the styles of questions possible. The questions are addressed to the team other than the one which devised them. Ask team members to all contribute to a prize: winners take all.

4   "Any questions?"

For team-taught courses/modules or joint sessions where two or more courses or modules come together. The team of lecturers form a panel. Students prepare questions of a broad and controversial nature concerning the subject. The process operates as for the BBC radio programme, with the audience encouraged to clap, hiss or boo less politely. "Any Questions?" can be valuable for instant synopses and to reveal differences between lecturers.

105

5   Students as teachers: I

List topics or concepts which need to be understood. Each student selects one item and agrees to learn enough to be able to teach it to someone else (preferably from another subject area or someone outside the Poly or an administrator). The student has to return with a signed affidavit to the effect that the 'audience' now understands the topic. This can be an assessed task.

6   Students as teachers: II

Students form groups of three. You select three topics/articles/problems which you want understood together with a test question for each topic. The students each work on one of the topics and then try to explain it to each of the other two (this need not take place in class). When they all come back together all students are tested on each of the three topics. Students gain the average mark obtained by the two students who they taught, rather than their own mark. In other words they are being assessed on whether they were able to learn *and teach* their topic adequately.

7   Student labs

Several weeks in advance, ask students, in groups of three, to design a lab session and submit their plans to you. You select the best plan and set the lab up to that design. The "winning" group have to brief their colleagues and explain their session design.

8   Student marking

Collect up the lab reports, or essays, or design work and redistribute it randomly to the class. Give some guidelines and criteria and then ask the students to mark and comment on the piece of work in front of them before giving it back to you to be returned to its author.

9   Guest lecture or seminar

Students choose who they would like to give a guest talk and what the topic of the talk should be. Provide information about possibilities e.g. specialisms of lecturers. Ask students for financial assistance should this be necessary.

10   Negotiate

Sit down with a small representative group of students, and this list of ideas, to co-operatively plan some changes in teaching and learning methods.

11   Student questions

Run a lecture or seminar by only speaking in response to student questions. Be really strict with yourself about not rambling off the point or using a question as an excuse to go over your favourite or prepared subjects. Be terse rather than verbose, as this will encourage follow-up questions.

12   Replan

Ask the students to redesign the course or module for next year's students, with a detailed breakdown of the subject matter as well as the processes and teaching methods. Groups should display their plans on posters or flipchart paper, selling their ideas. Compare and discuss plans in a workshop-type session and try to agree there and then to introducing at least some of the ideas.

13   Exam

Ask students to devise appropriate exam questions for the week. Discuss which are the best or most appropriate. Promise to use at least one of them at the end of the course.

14   Stop go

Allow students to stop you in lectures by simply raising a hand: no explanations necessary. When they have caught up with their notes, or formulated a question or whatever they needed the time for, they simply wave you on. In seminars students can stop the discussion, in order to enter it, by saying "BUZZ!".

15   Student-led seminars

All seminars are student-led are they not? Not when a lecturer chairs them they aren't. Try giving a student the role of chairing a seminar led by another student. If you still can't resist taking over then leave the room.

16   Student interviews

Involve experienced students in interviewing prospective students, and in open days for prospective applicants.

17   Interviewing staff

Involve experienced students in selection processes for new lecturing posts. Have candidates teach a small group and seek students' views about the candidate's competence at teaching.

18   Over to you

Give students a copy of this section of the book and ask them to devise other ideas for handing more control over to them.   Act on some of their suggestions.

LIBRARY